A VISIT TO THE ZOO!

Spanish Learning Book for Kids
Children's Foreign Language Books

BABY PROFESSOR
EDUCATION KIDS

The tiger is the biggest species of the cat family.

Tiger

Tiger Tigre

Koalas have sharp claws which help them climb trees.

Koala

Coala

There are currently 264 monkey species.

Monkey

Mono

Rhinoceros horns are made from a protein called keratin.

Rhinoceros

Rinoceronte

Male deer are called bucks. Females are called does.

Deer

Ciervo

The giraffe is the tallest mammal in the world.

Giraffe

Jirafa

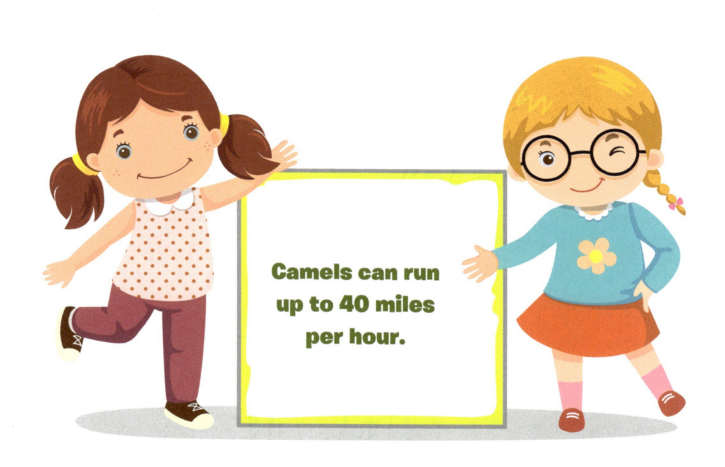

Camels can run up to 40 miles per hour.

Camel

Camello

Elephants are the largest land mammals.

Elephant

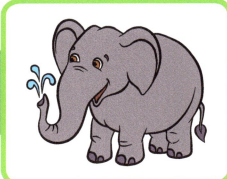

Elefante

Horses can sleep both lying down and standing up.

Horse

Caballo

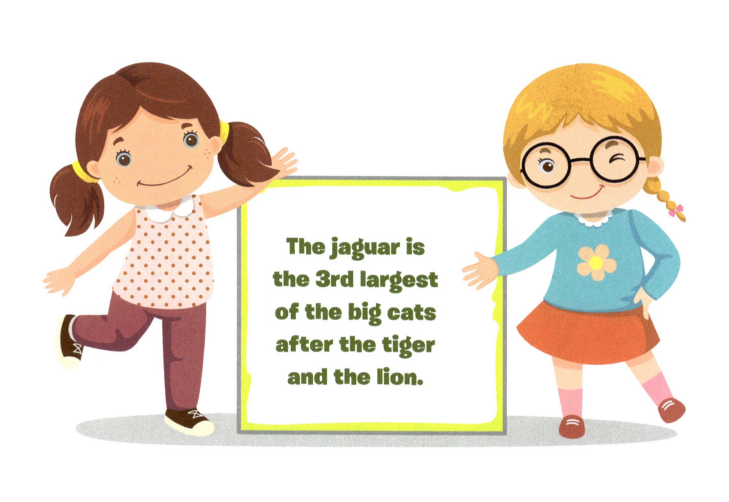

The jaguar is
the 3rd largest
of the big cats
after the tiger
and the lion.

Jaguar

Jaguar

Red pandas spend 13 hours a day eating.

Red Panda

Panda Rojo

Alpacas can live as long as 25 years and are able to survive in most climates.

Alpaca

Alpaca

Wolves are mammals and belong to the dog family.

Wolf

Lobo

Sloths can extend their tongues 10 to 12 inches out of their mouths.

Sloth

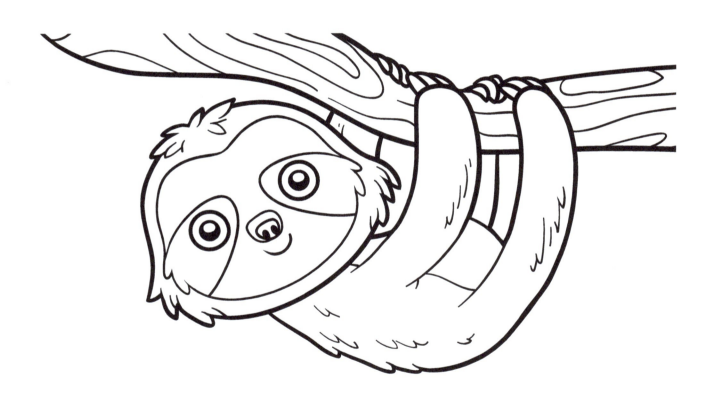

Perezoso

Kangaroos
are marsupial
animals that
are found in
Australia.

Kangaroo

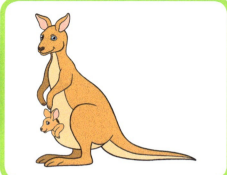

Canguro

Lions are the only cats that live in groups called prides.

Lion

León

The giant panda is native to China.

Panda

Panda

Snakes have flexible jaws which allow them to eat prey bigger than their head.

Snake

Serpiente

Hippopotamuses are found in Africa.

Hippopotamus

Hipopótamo

Crocodiles have the strongest bite of any animal in the world.

Crocodile

Cocodrilo

Tortoises can't swim, but they can hold their breath for a long time.

Tortoise

Tortuga

Walruses spend half their time on land and the other half in water.

Walrus

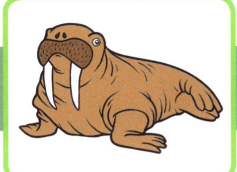

Morsa

Dolphins are believed to be very intelligent.

Dolphin

Delfín

Penguins
are flightless
birds.

Penguin

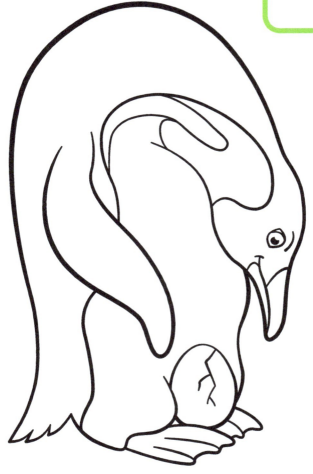

Pinguino

Owls have powerful talons which help them catch and kill prey.

Owl

Búho

An ostrich has the largest eye of any land mammal.

Ostrich

Avestruz

Peacocks can fly, but they stay on the ground most of the time.

Pavo real

Parrots are believed to be one of the most intelligent bird species.

Parrot

Loro

Toucans get most of their water from the fruit they eat.

Toucan

Tucán

Visit

BABY PROFESSOR
EDUCATION KIDS

www.BabyProfessorBooks.com

to download Free Baby Professor eBooks
and view our catalog of new and exciting
Children's Books

CPSIA information can be obtained
at www.ICGtesting.com
Printed in the USA
LVHW050733201122
733630LV00034B/1502